AMAZING ANIMALS

CONTENTS

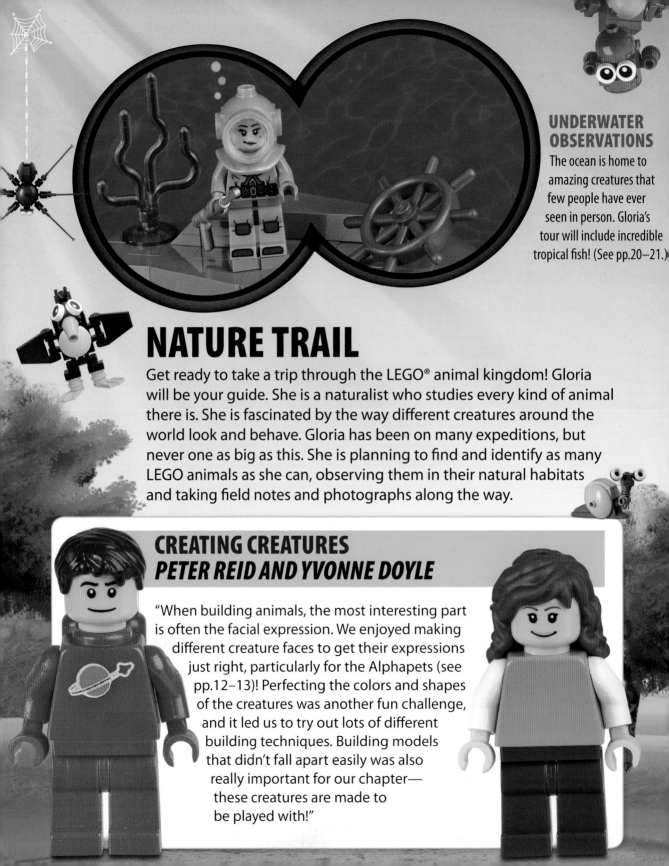

UNDERWATER OBSERVATIONS

The ocean is home to amazing creatures that few people have ever seen in person. Gloria's tour will include incredible tropical fish! (See pp.20–21.)

NATURE TRAIL

Get ready to take a trip through the LEGO® animal kingdom! Gloria will be your guide. She is a naturalist who studies every kind of animal there is. She is fascinated by the way different creatures around the world look and behave. Gloria has been on many expeditions, but never one as big as this. She is planning to find and identify as many LEGO animals as she can, observing them in their natural habitats and taking field notes and photographs along the way.

CREATING CREATURES
PETER REID AND YVONNE DOYLE

"When building animals, the most interesting part is often the facial expression. We enjoyed making different creature faces to get their expressions just right, particularly for the Alphapets (see pp.12–13)! Perfecting the colors and shapes of the creatures was another fun challenge, and it led us to try out lots of different building techniques. Building models that didn't fall apart easily was also really important for our chapter—these creatures are made to be played with!"

POLAR EXPLORATION

No location is too remote and no environment too extreme for this naturalist! Gloria will travel from the frozen Antarctic to the North Pole, meeting penguins, polar bears, and everything in between. (See pp.24–27.)

...AND BEYOND!

Not content to study only the animals she can find on Earth, Gloria will peer through a telescope to study strange creatures from other planets!

ON SAFARI

Kick off your animal adventure by going on an African safari! Put together a camouflaged lookout and keep watch to see what creatures wander past. Be very quiet and hold still—you don't want to scare the animals!

SAFARI... SO GOOD!

You could also build window covers to hide the lookout—or to give your minifigures some shade!

Place plants on a tan or yellow base to create a natural landscape

Use a step element or build a ladder to access the lookout

SIDE VIEW

1x2 log bricks look like side-by-side tree trunks

CAN YOU STAY ON THE STEPS, GLORIA? IT HELPS ATTRACT THE LIONS.

TREE-TOP HIDEAWAY

Palm leaves disguise the lookout's square plate roof so that the people inside won't be noticed by nearby animals. Flat and smooth shapes look artificial, so add some lumpy bits on top!

Use brown pieces so the structure blends in with the environment

LOOKOUT

On a safari you can go looking for animals, or you can wait for the animals to come to you. By building a lookout designed to blend in with the trees, your minifigures can observe the wildlife undetected.

Stilts can be 2x2 bricks or pairs of 1x2 bricks

Stilts keep the viewing platform out of reach of ground creatures

GIRAFFE

It's hard to overlook a giraffe out there on the savanna! With their long necks and legs, these towering titans really stand out in a crowd. Use 1x1 pieces to make the skinniest sections, and regular and inverted slopes for realistic angles.

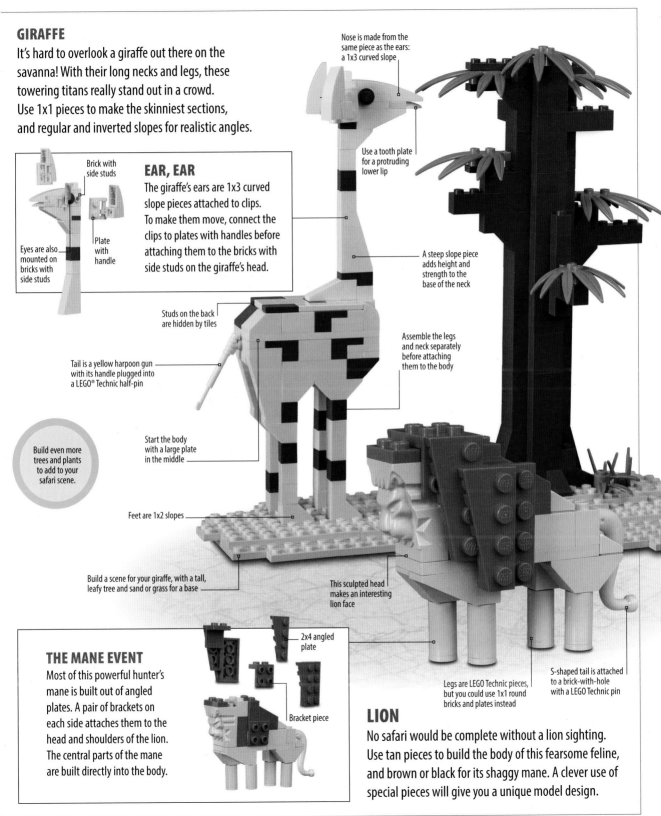

Brick with side studs

EAR, EAR

The giraffe's ears are 1x3 curved slope pieces attached to clips. To make them move, connect the clips to plates with handles before attaching them to the bricks with side studs on the giraffe's head.

Eyes are also mounted on bricks with side studs

Plate with handle

Nose is made from the same piece as the ears: a 1x3 curved slope

Use a tooth plate for a protruding lower lip

A steep slope piece adds height and strength to the base of the neck

Studs on the back are hidden by tiles

Assemble the legs and neck separately before attaching them to the body

Tail is a yellow harpoon gun with its handle plugged into a LEGO® Technic half-pin

Build even more trees and plants to add to your safari scene.

Start the body with a large plate in the middle

Feet are 1x2 slopes

Build a scene for your giraffe, with a tall, leafy tree and sand or grass for a base

This sculpted head makes an interesting lion face

THE MANE EVENT

Most of this powerful hunter's mane is built out of angled plates. A pair of brackets on each side attaches them to the head and shoulders of the lion. The central parts of the mane are built directly into the body.

2x4 angled plate

Bracket piece

Legs are LEGO Technic pieces, but you could use 1x1 round bricks and plates instead

S-shaped tail is attached to a brick-with-hole with a LEGO Technic pin

LION

No safari would be complete without a lion sighting. Use tan pieces to build the body of this fearsome feline, and brown or black for its shaggy mane. A clever use of special pieces will give you a unique model design.

SAFARI GIANTS

What giant-sized beasts will you see on your safari? You might spot a trumpeting elephant at the watering hole, an ostrich sprinting across the plains, or a herd of horned buffalo keeping an eye out for danger. Build them all for a grand wildlife adventure!

ELEPHANT

Elephants are the biggest animals you'll encounter on your expedition, so make sure you have plenty of gray bricks in your collection! Try starting your build with a six-stud-wide plate and building the body up from there.

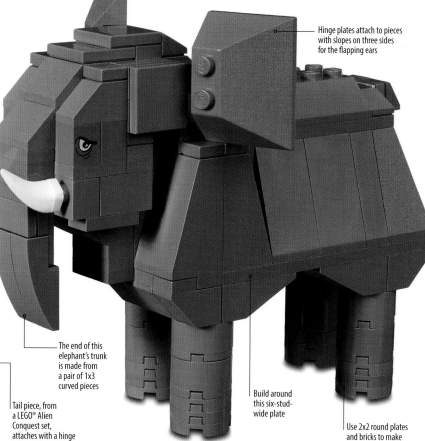

Hinge plates attach to pieces with slopes on three sides for the flapping ears

Use slope bricks to create the shape of the elephant's angled forehead

The end of this elephant's trunk is made from a pair of 1x3 curved pieces

Build around this six-stud-wide plate

Use 2x2 round plates and bricks to make the elephant's strong, pillar-like legs

SIDE VIEW

Attaching the legs last will make the rest of the body easier to build

Tail piece, from a LEGO® Alien Conquest set, attaches with a hinge brick so it's posable

---

⭐ CHALLENGE

ELEPHANT STAMPEDE

Challenge your friends to an elephant race! Put five bricks of different colors into a bag and take turns picking a brick from it. The color of the brick you pick determines which body part you can build for that turn. The winner is the first player to build a complete elephant.

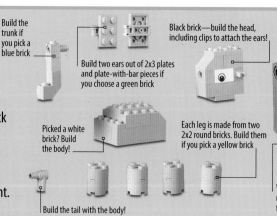

Build the trunk if you pick a blue brick

Build two ears out of 2x3 plates and plate-with-bar pieces if you choose a green brick

Black brick—build the head, including clips to attach the ears!

Picked a white brick? Build the body!

Each leg is made from two 2x2 round bricks. Build them if you pick a yellow brick

Build the tail with the body!

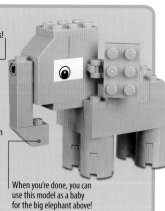

When you're done, you can use this model as a baby for the big elephant above!

Beak is a skeleton leg from a LEGO® Ninjago™ set

YOU CAN'T RUFFLE MY FEATHERS—THEY'RE PLASTIC!

Center of the head is a 1x1 brick with studs on four sides

OSTRICH

These large, flightless birds are extremely fast runners, so give your model a pair of long, straight legs. Make sure your ostrich's body is well balanced so it doesn't fall over. Female ostriches are brown or gray—why not use your pieces in those colors to build a female version?

1x1 slope piece

Tooth plate

BIG BIRD BODY

Use plates and inverted slopes to build the ostrich's lower body, with 1x1 slopes for its raised, feathery back. Attach tooth plates to brackets on both sides to create the wings. Another tooth plate is used for the tail feathers.

Stack orange, tan, or pink 1x1 round plates to make the neck

Legs are telescopes, and two-toed feet are 1x1 plates with side clips

What other safari animals can you build to add to your safari scene?

2x3 angled plate

BUILD-A-BUFFALO

A pair of bricks with two side studs holds the whole model together on the inside. Angled plates attach to them sideways to create the buffalo's thick hide, and grilles make the hair of its shaggy coat.

Long curved bricks create a true-to-nature humpbacked shape

Bricks with side studs

1x2 grille

BUFFALO

Don't be tricked by its cow-like appearance—the buffalo is as short-tempered and tough as they come! Build as many as you can and create a whole herd of these majestic, but grumpy, beasts to populate your safari scenes.

The buffalo's eyes are headlight bricks

Horns from a LEGO cow plug into headlight bricks with hollow side studs

Plates with click hinges let the head hang at an angle

Use tooth plates to create short, sharp hooves peeking out from under the hair

BARNYARD BEASTS

Expand your farm and build animals that baa, bray, moo, or neigh! They will all need their own place to live and food to eat, so do a bit of research before you build. How else will you know how to take proper care of them all?

COUNTING THESE SHEEP MAKES ME FEEL SLEEPY... YAWN!

Sheep like to munch on low-growing plants

Make a fence out of bar or antenna pieces attached to 1x1 bricks with side studs

SHEEP PEN

When building a sheep pen, use a green base plate so your sheep have plenty of fresh grass for grazing. If you have enough pieces, build the fence all the way around and add a gate so that the farmer can get inside.

Build smaller, simpler versions of your sheep to make lambs—or skinny pink versions for shearing season!

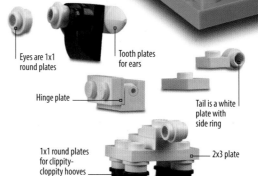

Eyes are 1x1 round plates

Tooth plates for ears

Hinge plate

Tail is a white plate with side ring

1x1 round plates for clippity-cloppity hooves

2x3 plate

SHEEP

Want to make a woolly sheep? Start with a 2x3 plate and attach a hinge for the neck. Plates with side rings sticking out create a thick and curly coat.

COWS

Add a couple of cows to your farm scene. Use contrasting black and white pieces to create their patchy hides. A cow's wide back can be made with a curved 2x4 brick and a droid torso piece is just the right shape for its head!

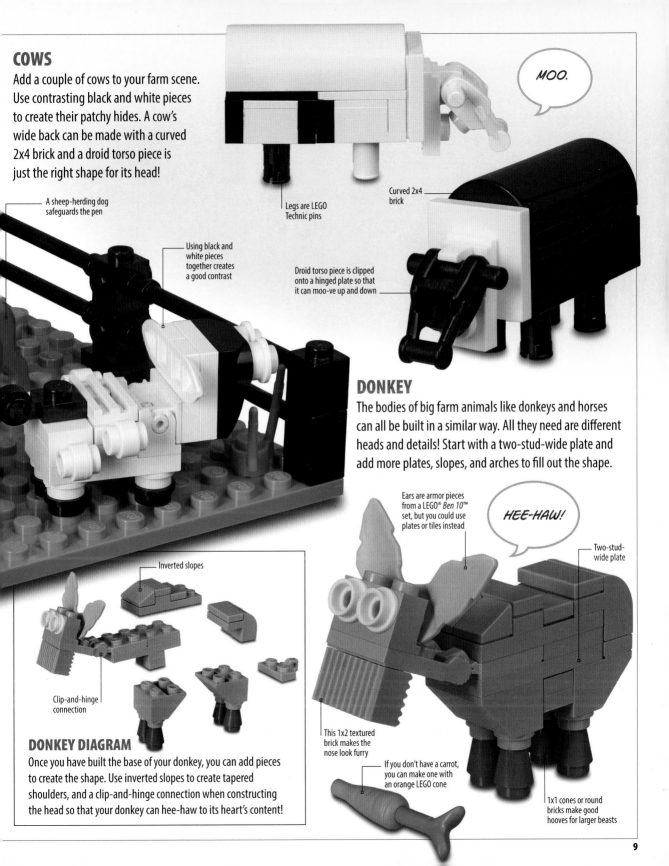

MOO.

A sheep-herding dog safeguards the pen

Using black and white pieces together creates a good contrast

Legs are LEGO Technic pins

Curved 2x4 brick

Droid torso piece is clipped onto a hinged plate so that it can moo-ve up and down

DONKEY

The bodies of big farm animals like donkeys and horses can all be built in a similar way. All they need are different heads and details! Start with a two-stud-wide plate and add more plates, slopes, and arches to fill out the shape.

Ears are armor pieces from a LEGO® Ben 10™ set, but you could use plates or tiles instead

HEE-HAW!

Two-stud-wide plate

Inverted slopes

Clip-and-hinge connection

DONKEY DIAGRAM

Once you have built the base of your donkey, you can add pieces to create the shape. Use inverted slopes to create tapered shoulders, and a clip-and-hinge connection when constructing the head so that your donkey can hee-haw to its heart's content!

This 1x2 textured brick makes the nose look furry

If you don't have a carrot, you can make one with an orange LEGO cone

1x1 cones or round bricks make good hooves for larger beasts

FARM FOWL

You don't have to travel too far afield to discover interesting animals. Take a trip to the farm and you will find cows, pigs, horses, and much more—not to mention the different kinds of birds that live there. Let's meet a few of our most familiar and favorite feathered friends.

DUCK POND

Ducks love water, so build a pond on your farm where they can quack and splash to their hearts' content. Ponds can be found anywhere, surrounded by grass or in the dirt. You could also add some frogs or fishy friends to your pond!

Use colorless transparent tiles for a frozen winter pond!

QUICK BUILD

Tile for a smooth body

1x1 brick with studs on four sides

1x1 cone for a tail

Wings are tooth plates

Head is a fire hose nozzle

DUCKS

These little ducks are made with just seven pieces. Start with a 1x1 brick with studs on four sides, and attach a tail, wings, and a clip to hold the head.

DON'T MIND ME, GUYS. JUST ACT NATURAL!

Make a still water surface with transparent blue tiles

Place plants at the edge of the pond or sticking out of the water

Ducks can perch on the side or go for a swim

Build a ring of gray plates for stone, or brown for mud, around the pond

CHICKEN COOP

Your chickens will need to be protected from foxes and other predators, so build a coop to keep them (and their precious eggs) safe.

I'M FEELING COOPED UP IN HERE.

Grilles give the impression of a feathery back

Ice cream cone tops or 1x1 round plates make egg-cellent eggs!

Use small plates to make straw bedding

If you don't have these latticed fences, any fence pieces will do

You could build a fence all the way around so your chickens don't get out, and nothing else gets in!

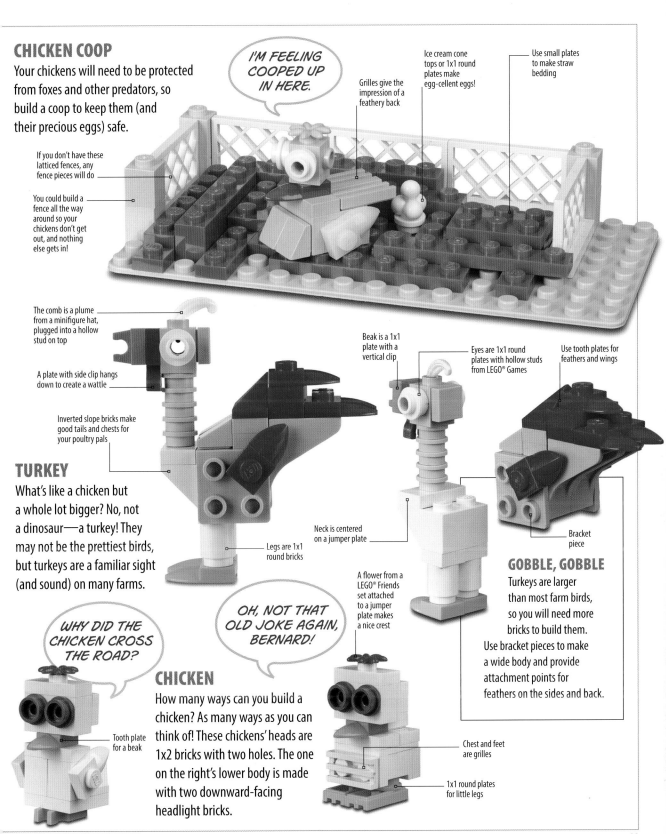

The comb is a plume from a minifigure hat, plugged into a hollow stud on top

A plate with side clip hangs down to create a wattle

Inverted slope bricks make good tails and chests for your poultry pals

Beak is a 1x1 plate with a vertical clip

Eyes are 1x1 round plates with hollow studs from LEGO® Games

Use tooth plates for feathers and wings

TURKEY

What's like a chicken but a whole lot bigger? No, not a dinosaur—a turkey! They may not be the prettiest birds, but turkeys are a familiar sight (and sound) on many farms.

Legs are 1x1 round bricks

Neck is centered on a jumper plate

A flower from a LEGO® Friends set attached to a jumper plate makes a nice crest

Bracket piece

GOBBLE, GOBBLE

Turkeys are larger than most farm birds, so you will need more bricks to build them. Use bracket pieces to make a wide body and provide attachment points for feathers on the sides and back.

WHY DID THE CHICKEN CROSS THE ROAD?

OH, NOT THAT OLD JOKE AGAIN, BERNARD!

Tooth plate for a beak

CHICKEN

How many ways can you build a chicken? As many ways as you can think of! These chickens' heads are 1x2 bricks with two holes. The one on the right's lower body is made with two downward-facing headlight bricks.

Chest and feet are grilles

1x1 round plates for little legs

11

ALPHAPETS

Building these peculiar little creatures is as easy as A-B-C! You can make all sorts of strange, silly, and unusual animal faces by using LEGO tiles with printed numbers and letters. If you don't have these decorated tiles, then try other ones with interesting patterns and colors from your collection.

With two Q tiles and an upside-down Y, this cat looks curious and hopeful

Use tooth plates for pointy, triangular ears

Two V tiles and a P tile create scrunched up eyes and a tongue sticking out!

Back can be a slope or a curved brick

HERE, BIRDIE! TWEET, TWEET!

CATS

Use different letters to give your crouching kitty a new expression! Even without letter tiles, you can use pieces with printed grilles or dials to change your creation's face and mood.

Red hinge plate creates a cat's collar

Four tooth plates make the front and hind feet

Base of body is a 2x3 plate

What other animals could you add to your Alphapet collection?

A hinge base lets the head tilt up and down

PET PIECES

Think about how to use your pieces in different ways, like tilting a tooth plate to create a floppy ear. Experiment with your pieces and you'll discover lots of ways to fill your creations with heaps of fun.

Use pieces with side studs to build in different directions

Angle the ears back to make the pup look like it's running

A grille creates a fuzzy white chest

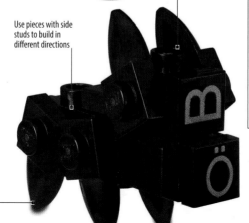

Use sideways tooth plates for stubby little legs

BIRD

Sometimes you find the perfect piece to make an animal part. This bird's wings are a pair of LEGO minifigure fan accessories, plugged into 1x1 plates with side rings.

Letter Ö tiles give this bird a wide-eyed look

Fluttering wings can twist in their rings and rotate on the body's side studs

1x1 brick with side studs

BIRD BODY

Birds come in many shapes. The head and body of this bird is built around a pair of 1x1 bricks with studs on four sides.

Plate with side ring

Neck is a 1x2 plate. Use a longer plate for a longer neck

Beak is a horn plugged into a hollow stud

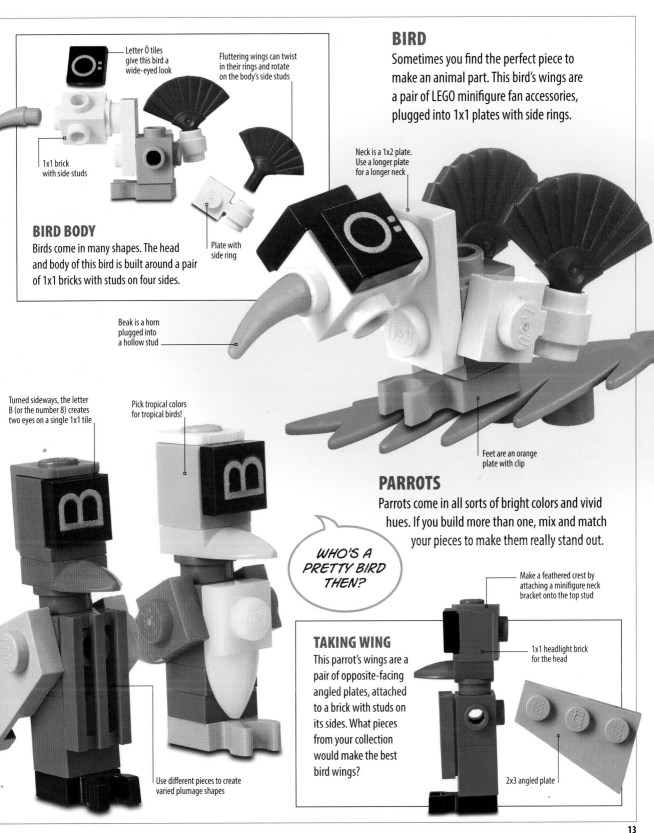

Feet are an orange plate with clip

Turned sideways, the letter B (or the number 8) creates two eyes on a single 1x1 tile

Pick tropical colors for tropical birds!

PARROTS

Parrots come in all sorts of bright colors and vivid hues. If you build more than one, mix and match your pieces to make them really stand out.

WHO'S A PRETTY BIRD THEN?

Make a feathered crest by attaching a minifigure neck bracket onto the top stud

TAKING WING

This parrot's wings are a pair of opposite-facing angled plates, attached to a brick with studs on its sides. What pieces from your collection would make the best bird wings?

1x1 headlight brick for the head

2x3 angled plate

Use different pieces to create varied plumage shapes

CREEPING CRITTERS

Just look at these darlings, with all of their legs and eyes and mandibles and antennae. Build some bugs and grubs, and spiders and centipedes—these little critters can be cute, too! Show how much you love them by building the creepiest crawlies you can imagine.

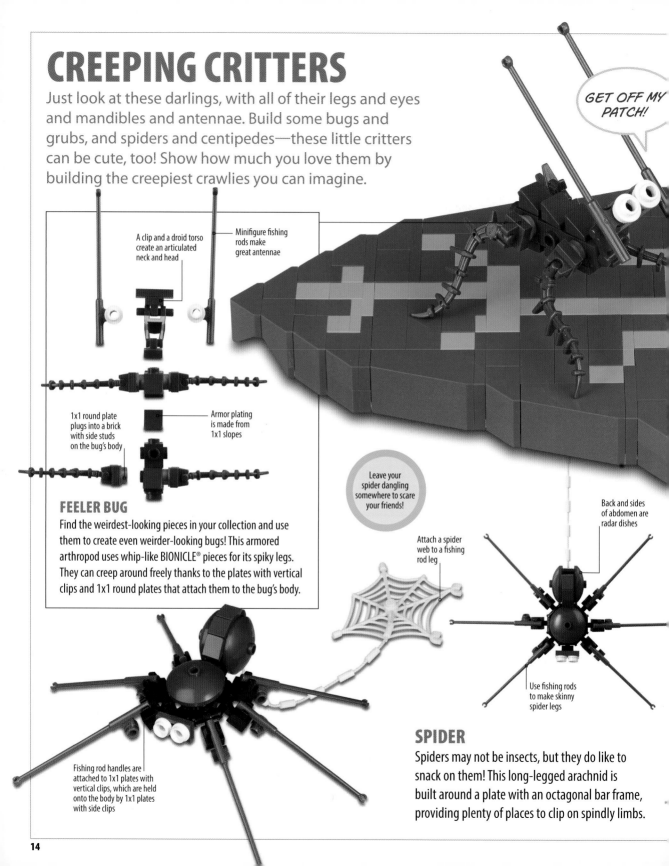

GET OFF MY PATCH!

A clip and a droid torso create an articulated neck and head

Minifigure fishing rods make great antennae

1x1 round plate plugs into a brick with side studs on the bug's body

Armor plating is made from 1x1 slopes

FEELER BUG

Find the weirdest-looking pieces in your collection and use them to create even weirder-looking bugs! This armored arthropod uses whip-like BIONICLE® pieces for its spiky legs. They can creep around freely thanks to the plates with vertical clips and 1x1 round plates that attach them to the bug's body.

Leave your spider dangling somewhere to scare your friends!

Attach a spider web to a fishing rod leg

Back and sides of abdomen are radar dishes

Use fishing rods to make skinny spider legs

Fishing rod handles are attached to 1x1 plates with vertical clips, which are held onto the body by 1x1 plates with side clips

SPIDER

Spiders may not be insects, but they do like to snack on them! This long-legged arachnid is built around a plate with an octagonal bar frame, providing plenty of places to clip on spindly limbs.

14

CENTIPEDE

When constructing a long critter like this centipede, build a chain of identical body sections—as many as you want! Give each section a pair of legs so it can stand up and scurry.

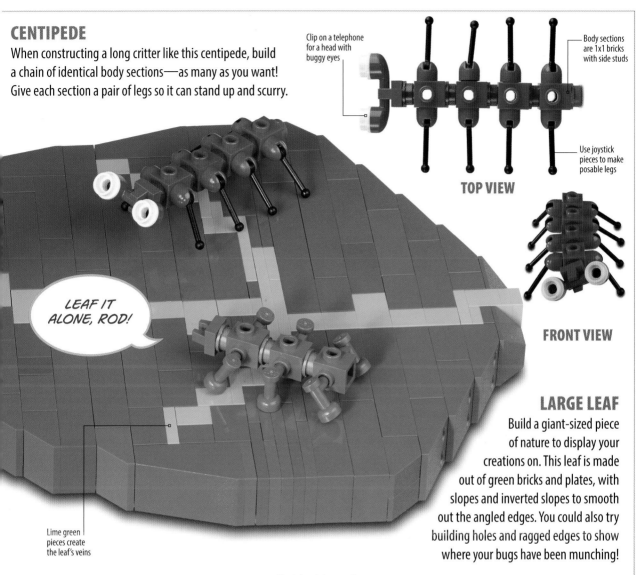

Clip on a telephone for a head with buggy eyes

Body sections are 1x1 bricks with side studs

Use joystick pieces to make posable legs

TOP VIEW

FRONT VIEW

LEAF IT ALONE, ROD!

Lime green pieces create the leaf's veins

LARGE LEAF

Build a giant-sized piece of nature to display your creations on. This leaf is made out of green bricks and plates, with slopes and inverted slopes to smooth out the angled edges. You could also try building holes and ragged edges to show where your bugs have been munching!

GREEN BUG

This skittering critter is built entirely out of small LEGO pieces. Its segments are made from 1x1 bricks with side studs, and 1x1 round plates in between.

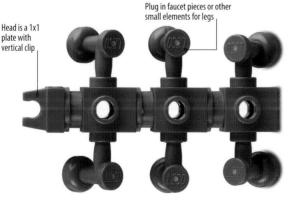

Head is a 1x1 plate with vertical clip

Plug in faucet pieces or other small elements for legs

TOP VIEW

COOL BRICK

"This 1x1 brick with studs on top and four sides allows you to build outwards in lots of directions. It's a great brick for an animal head or the center of a body."

15

MORE CREEPING CRITTERS

There are lots of other invertebrates out there that you can build! Just look under a rock, up a tree, or in a garden and you're sure to find all sorts of creeping, crawling, slithering, and slimy creatures to inspire your creativity.

SNAILS

Snails may not be the fastest critters around, but these ones are quick builds if you have the right parts. You could also make a slug by leaving off the shell part!

WAIT UP! YOU'RE GOING TOO FAST!

SNAIL SHELL

A snail's shell is its home, so take care when building this part! The center of the snail's shell is a 1x1 brick with side studs. Radar dishes attach to the 1x1 brick's side studs.

You could use radar dish pieces in any color

Small radar dish fits under the larger radar dish

1x1 brick with side studs

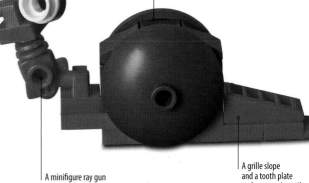

Eyestalks are a telephone handset on a clip

A minifigure ray gun creates a detailed, angled neck

A grille slope and a tooth plate make a tapering tail

▶ QUICK BUILD

LADYBUGS

You can build a little ladybug out of just seven pieces. For a bigger challenge, try to change the design so that your ladybug is flying!

Body is two dome bricks held together by a small LEGO Technic axle

Use a plate with a vertical clip for mandibles

Head is a black 1x1 brick with four side studs

Gaps in shell look like a ladybug's black spots!

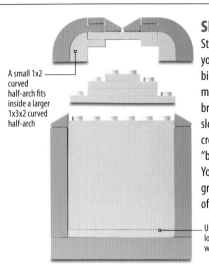

SLICED BREAD

Start the construction of your bread slice with a big white wall in the middle. Use tan or brown bricks for the crust. 1x1 slopes and arch bricks create the distinctive "bread" shape at the top. You could also add some green bricks for a touch of mold!

A small 1x2 curved half-arch fits inside a larger 1x3x2 curved half-arch

Use one big wall element or stack lots of white bricks to form the white part of the bread slice

SHOO, FLY!

To make the body of this fly, use three 1x1 bricks with studs on four sides. For the head, use another 1x1 brick with side studs, but in a different color.

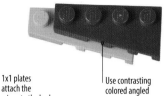

1x1 plates attach the wings to the body

Use contrasting colored angled plates for the wings

Eyes are decorated 1x1 round tiles from a LEGO Ninjago set

Robot-claw legs plug into hollow studs

Why stop at one fly? Build a whole swarm!

FLY AND BREAD

If you leave food out long enough, you are sure to attract some buzzing company. A slice of bread makes an inviting landing pad for a hungry fly—and it might even bring some friends!

A FEAST FIT FOR A FLY!

A minifigure pickax makes a terrific insect proboscis!

Each wing is made from two small angled plates

Use robot claws for the legs

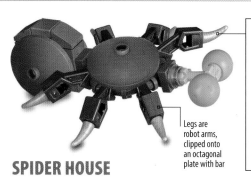

SPIDER BELLY

To make the sides of this armored abdomen, attach small radar dishes to bricks with side studs, then add larger radar dishes over the small ones.

The spider's mandibles are horn pieces

LEGO Technic ball joints make great spider eyes

Attach LEGO Technic balls to a shaft piece

Brick with side studs

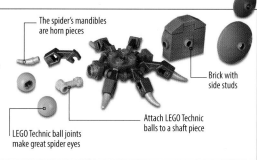

Legs are robot arms, clipped onto an octagonal plate with bar

SPIDER HOUSE

Many zoos are home to different species of spiders and other invertebrates. Build some creepy-crawler creations for your zoo.

AT THE ZOO

A zoo is a marvelous place to see creatures from all over the world in one location. Think about what will keep your zoo animals happy, like an enclosure with climbing bars to monkey around on and trees to climb.

Use transparent 1x1 round tiles for eyes that look like they're glowing

This bug variation uses a second octagonal plate with bar for its abdomen

A 1x1 round stud supports the radar dish on top

CHECK OUT MY "WEB" SITE!

Body and head are both 1x1 bricks with studs on four sides

A minifigure pistol plugs into a cone to create a slender tail

A horn provides a beak for drinking nectar from flowers

Sometimes a model's color scheme is dictated by its special parts. These fans are only made in red and black...so far!

HUMMINGBIRD

A hummingbird is small and light, so you don't have to use a lot of bricks to build its body. LEGO minifigure fans make perfect rapidly beating wings.

SNAKE

The joints of this super-posable snake are made from droid torsos, with segments assembled from side-stud bricks, small plates, and plates with vertical clips. If you don't have enough parts to build a snake this long, build a shorter one!

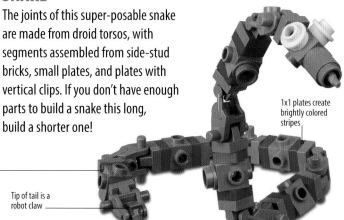

1x1 plates create brightly colored stripes

HISSING SNAKE

The snake's head is a 1x1 brick with four side studs. A round brick is used for a nose and its hissing tongue is a unicorn's horn!

Round brick

A droid torso connects the head to the first segment of the body

Tip of tail is a robot claw

MONKEY

Monkeys are always up to something, so let them play by giving them different head and limb positions. This one is designed to sit on the ground. Its head is built upside down to give it a cheeky and whimsical expression!

Top of head is a 2x2 slide plate from underneath a boat

Use plates with side rings to make the monkey's ears

One 2x2 dome gives the monkey's snout a little round mouth, and another gives it a bellybutton!

Eyes are attached to headlight bricks

MONKEY BUSINESS

To make this cheeky monkey's head, use a 2x2 dome connected to bricks with side studs. If you don't have plates with printed eyes, any 1x1 round pieces will do!

Hinge plates allow its legs to swing out to the sides

Climbing bars built out of LEGO Technic bricks and long bar elements

Arms are LEGO® Minifigure ray guns

This small tree is built with bricks, small plant leaves, and regular and inverted slopes

This monkey's legs are 1x2 curved half-arches, and its feet are tooth plates

MONKEY PEN

You can build an animal enclosure out of bricks, fence pieces, or even a ring of clipped-together ladders. Fill your zoo displays with objects that will keep the animals inside exercised and entertained.

A rubber auto tire can provide hours of interaction for a curious primate

WHAT'S THAT, GLORIA? WHY OF COURSE YOU CAN HAVE A BANANA!

Plates with vertical clips make hands that can hold onto objects

OOO! OO!

TROPICAL FISH

Strap on a snorkel and check out these eye-catching underwater fish! Some sea creatures are patterned to blend in with their environments, but not these flashy fellows. Their vivid colorations stand out from the crowd. Use your most colorful bricks to make some tropical fish friends of your own.

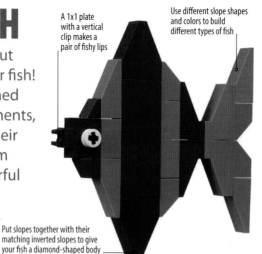

A 1x1 plate with a vertical clip makes a pair of fishy lips

Use different slope shapes and colors to build different types of fish

Put slopes together with their matching inverted slopes to give your fish a diamond-shaped body

AXLE-EYED FISH

Here's a novel way to make fish eyes! Build a 1x2 LEGO Technic brick with a cross-shaped hole into the head, then slide a short cross-axle through and add a half-bush on each side.

CLOWNFISH

Do you have a lot of orange bricks and slopes? Then build a cheerful clownfish! Except for the eyes and fins, its brightly hued body is built like a wall and entirely flat. Its body is very narrow, so attach its left fin higher than the one on its right. By putting the left fin's own click hinge plate lower than the right fin's, you will even both sides out.

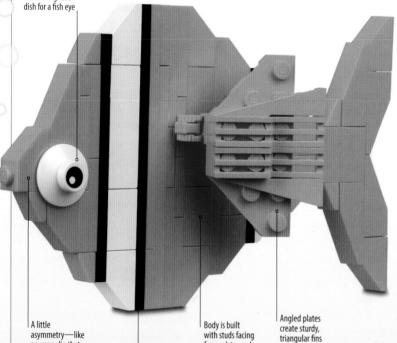

Attach a 1x1 round plate or tile to a big radar dish for a fish eye

A little asymmetry—like an upper lip that sticks out—gives a fish more character

Create thin black stripes with plates and thick white stripes with bricks

Body is built with studs facing forward, toward the head

Angled plates create sturdy, triangular fins

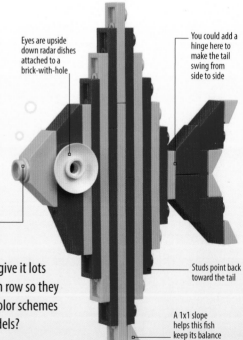

Eyes are upside down radar dishes attached to a brick-with-hole

You could add a hinge here to make the tail swing from side to side

Mouth is a 1x1 round plate plugged into the bottom of an inverted slope

Studs point back toward the tail

A 1x1 slope helps this fish keep its balance

STRIPY FISH

Build a fish's body entirely out of plates to give it lots of skinny stripes. Stagger the plates in each row so they all stay locked together. What other wild color schemes can you come up with for your marine models?

Build top fins out of slopes, plates, and tiles

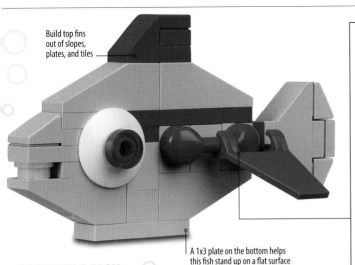

Radar-dish eye also attaches to a brick with side studs

Telephone handset

Brick with side studs

Flag piece

FISH FIN

To make this fish's fin, attach a telephone handset to bricks with side studs that are built into the fish's body. Clip a flag onto the telephone's handle to make a fin that can move up and down as the fish swims.

A 1x3 plate on the bottom helps this fish stand up on a flat surface

GRINNING FISH

A 1x1 plate inside its mouth gives this odd fish a round-toothed smile. A transparent red tile attached to a radar dish for an eye adds to its strange appearance!

SMALL FISH

Use little slopes to build a little fish. Small slopes give your model all kinds of interesting angled shapes and patterns.

Eye is a 1x1 round plate plugged into a 1x1 brick-with-hole

Use two 1x3 slopes to make the tail

WHY ARE FISH SO SMART?

Side fins are held on by brackets

BECAUSE WE ARE ALWAYS IN A SCHOOL!

Radar dish eyes are held in place by a 1x1 brick with studs on two sides

BIG-HEADED FISH

Not every fish has to be made out of straight lines and angles. Use curved bricks to add smooth, rounded features to your aquatic creations. Curved pieces also make a fish look graceful and streamlined.

The body is built from the bottom up, starting with a 1x6 plate

MADE-UP CREATURES

Imagine discovering a creature that no one has ever seen before. What would it look like? Maybe it's something totally alien that could never possibly exist on our planet. What kinds of made-up creatures can you build with your bricks?

Head is one giant eyeball made from two radar dishes, held together by a pulley wheel

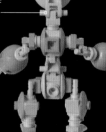

"The ray gun is a space weapon, but it's used here as part of the dancing alien's leg! You will also see it used as part of a snail's head (p.16) and a monkey's elbow (p.19)."

I'VE GOT MY EYE ON YOU!

Lower arms are 2x2 domes connected with a short LEGO Technic cross-axle

Fire hose nozzles attached to clips give the shoulders and hips plenty of movement

Build the arms and legs first before attaching them to the main body

A droid torso and a clip create a posable neck to attach the head to the body

ALIEN OBSERVER

Play with shapes and proportions. This creature may have two arms, two legs, and a head, just like humans do, but the way those body parts are built makes it very different indeed.

Top and bottom body sections are built around 1x1 bricks with studs on four sides, with a droid torso in between

REAR VIEW

LASER LEGS

Two ray guns with a faucet element in the middle make up each leg. The ray guns' handles plug into hollow studs on the body and feet.

A small transparent radar dish over a larger white one creates a wide, staring eye

DANCING GOOFBALL

Here's another creature with a big eye, but that's where the similarities end. With its strong legs and suction-cup feet, it must come from a world with really low gravity!

Multi-jointed neck is built out of plates with clips and handles

Body is an octagonal plate with bar, covered by a radar dish

Faucet piece

Brown radar dishes make alien shoes that are built for dancing!

REAR VIEW

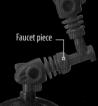

BLUE BOUNCER

This alien creature loves to hop around on its frog-like feet. Everything it meets is a delightful surprise—that's why its eyes and mouth are so round!

How do you make the eyes stick up in a V-formation? Just rotate the 1x1 brick with four side studs at the back!

Eyestalks are paddles plugged into 1x1 cones

Eyes are made with transparent round tiles, white radar dishes, and paddles

Legs are made with 1x1 plates and faucet elements

REAR VIEW

Flippers make great imaginary creature feet

Mouth is a 1x1 round plate

...es for ...h and ...dy details

GARDEN GREEB

Nobody knows where this creature came from, but it sure hates it when you forget to water the garden. Make sure it gets plenty of sunlight to help it grow!

1x3 plates make feet that are perfectly camouflaged for standing near carrots!

Yellow socks made from pairs of 1x1 round plates

CREATURE-CREATION

The head of this strange alien is a 1x1 brick with four side studs, with bulging eyes made from hollow-stud LEGO Games round plates. The body is a 2x2 dome on top of a 2x2 round plate. Its snow shoe feet connect to the body with 1x1 round plates.

A 1x1 round plate also attaches the alien's hat to its head

2x2 round plate

UNDERCOVER ALIENS

Even if you only have a few pieces, you can still make a wild and wacky alien creature. Build a whole crew and give them different hats to help them blend in on Earth. Use a minifigure hat, or simply a small cone or round brick.

Cap from a lumberjack in the LEGO Minifigure series

A small cone makes a great fez!

Clown bowler hat from the LEGO Minifigures series

I HAVE A UNIQUE STYLE.

...se minifigure ...ppers or ...ow shoes for ...apping feet

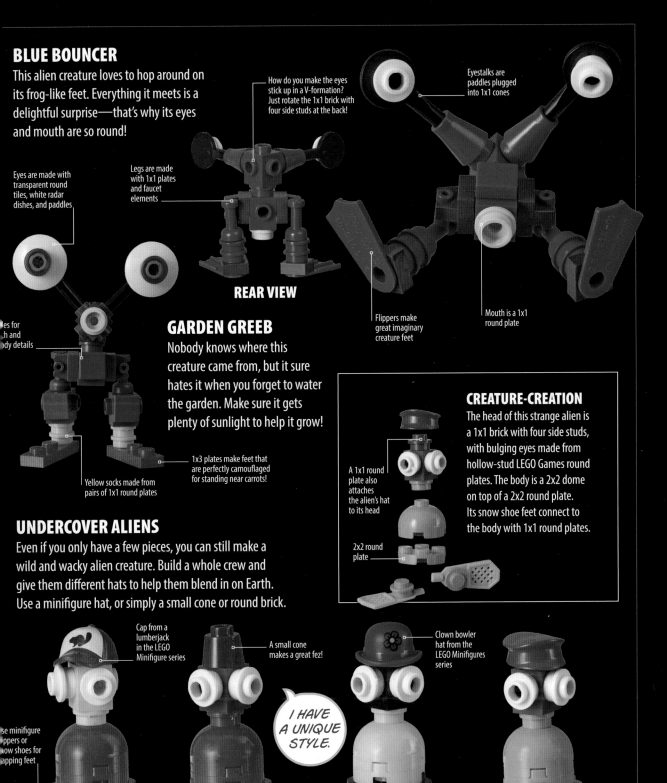

AT THE POLES

If you think winter is tough where you live, try living in the Arctic or the Antarctic! The animals there have to be tough, hardy, and well-insulated against the cold. Build an icy polar scene and some creatures to fill it, but be warned—you may need to use all of your white bricks!

When building a background, add higher ridges to create far-off hills and snow banks

POLAR PEAKS

Use your micro-scale building skills to make a miniature background for your icy scene. A mixture of white and gray pieces creates a stark and atmospheric snow-capped mountain vista.

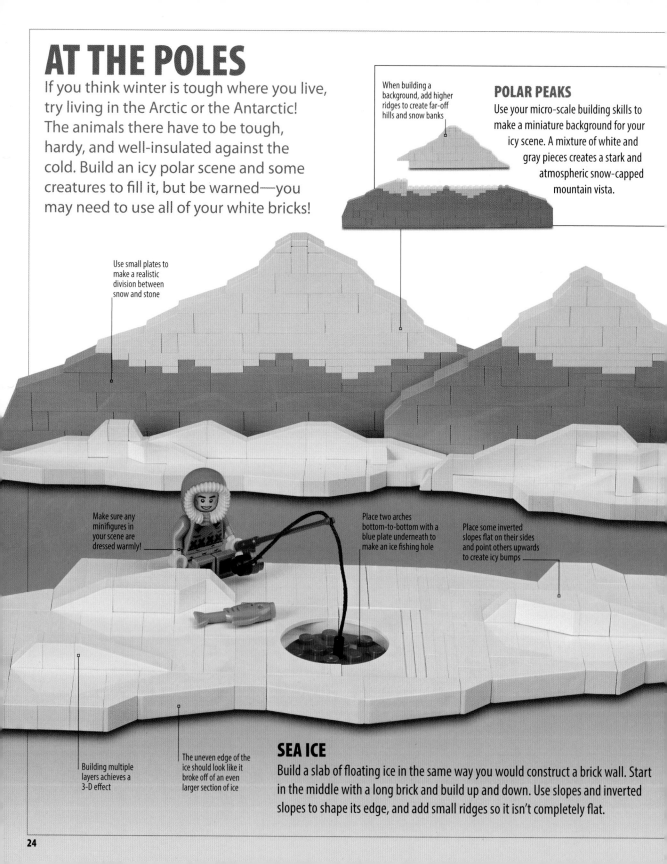

Use small plates to make a realistic division between snow and stone

Make sure any minifigures in your scene are dressed warmly!

Place two arches bottom-to-bottom with a blue plate underneath to make an ice fishing hole

Place some inverted slopes flat on their sides and point others upwards to create icy bumps

Building multiple layers achieves a 3-D effect

The uneven edge of the ice should look like it broke off of an even larger section of ice

SEA ICE

Build a slab of floating ice in the same way you would construct a brick wall. Start in the middle with a long brick and build up and down. Use slopes and inverted slopes to shape its edge, and add small ridges so it isn't completely flat.

PENGUINS

Start your penguin with a 1x1 brick with studs on all four sides. Add a round plate for a neck, black tooth plates for wings, and 1x2 tiles in front and back.

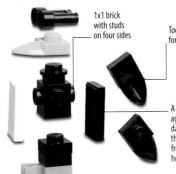

1x1 brick with studs on four sides

Tooth plate for wings

A black back against deep, dark water hides the penguin from predators hunting above

Why not add an igloo to keep your minifigures warm on cold polar nights?

y including bricks with de studs in your ice slab wall, you can attach the ountains as vertical walls

Binoculars make keen eyes for spotting fish

Baby penguins are covered in fuzzy down to keep them warm until they are grown-up

One-stud connections let you swivel and pose the head and wings

Use a tooth plate for a pointy beak

Feet are a single 1x1 plate with side clip

Use a 1x1 round tile for a penguin chick's belly

MUSH, DOGGIES! WE'VE GOT TO GET HOME BEFORE RUSH HOUR!

DOG SLED

Move over, snowmobile—out here on the polar ice, canine power is the way to travel! Start your dog sled with a 2x4 plate and attach a pair of runners for smooth movement over snow.

If you don't have hockey sticks for runners, use poles or bars instead

You could add a longer section at the back for carrying important supplies

An angled front cuts down on wind resistance for faster speed

Round plates on the end of string elements attach to studs on the backs of LEGO dogs

ARCTIC ANIMALS

To see the wildest animals on the planet, you've got to travel to the ends of Earth. Here at the North Pole, it's eat or be eaten…and few creatures are as good at eating as these ones! Build some ferocious predators to fill your polar scene. What other cold-weather animals could you build?

KILLER WHALE

To build this mighty killer whale's streamlined body, start in the middle with a long, two-stud-wide black brick or plate. Use white pieces for its stomach and a patch on its body.

Add 1x1 round plates for the top teeth, too

Hinge plate

CHILLY CHOMPERS

The killer whale's mouth is full of 1x1 round plate teeth, surrounding a pink tile tongue. Its upper jaw is attached with a hinge so it can open and close for a great big chomp.

If you build a bigger killer whale model, you could use cones as pointy teeth!

Attach the white section under the jaws with jumper plates

Use jumper plates to center a dorsal fin, built from slope and curved bricks

Use arches to build the rounded snout

The whale's eyes are transparent 1x1 round plates attached to headlight bricks

WHY CAN'T THERE BE PENGUINS ON MY PAGE?

ARCTIC HARE

Arctic hares may not be the meanest creatures around, but they're great at surviving. Hide one in your polar scene and see if anybody notices!

Minifigure neck brackets hold the ears in position

This printed 1x2 brick comes from a LEGO® Creator set, but you could also build your own hare face

Use tooth plates for feet and long ears

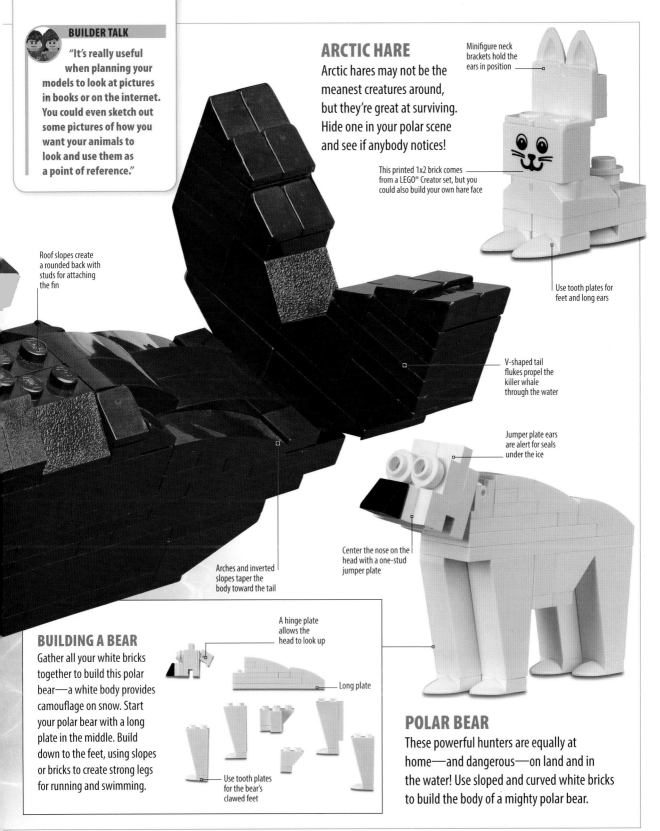

Roof slopes create a rounded back with studs for attaching the fin

V-shaped tail flukes propel the killer whale through the water

Jumper plate ears are alert for seals under the ice

Center the nose on the head with a one-stud jumper plate

Arches and inverted slopes taper the body toward the tail

BUILDING A BEAR

Gather all your white bricks together to build this polar bear—a white body provides camouflage on snow. Start your polar bear with a long plate in the middle. Build down to the feet, using slopes or bricks to create strong legs for running and swimming.

A hinge plate allows the head to look up

Long plate

Use tooth plates for the bear's clawed feet

POLAR BEAR

These powerful hunters are equally at home—and dangerous—on land and in the water! Use sloped and curved white bricks to build the body of a mighty polar bear.

HANDFUL OF BRICKS LIST

4x4 plate x 1

2x2 inverted slope x 1

2x2 brick x 3

2 x 4 brick x 2

2x2 plate x 2

1x2/1x4 angle plate x1

1x6 plate x 2

2x2 slope x 3

Antenna x1

1x2 slope x 2

2x3 slope x 1

1x1 slope x 4

1x1 brick eyes x 2

1x2 tile with top bar x 1

1x2 plate x 1

1x1 round brick x 1

2x4 angled plate x 2

1x2 curved half-arch x 1

4x4 round plate x 1

2x2 round brick x 1

For DK Publishing
Project Editor Hannah Dolan
Senior Designer Guy Harvey
Editors Jo Casey, Matt Jones, Victoria Taylor
Designers Jill Bunyan, Sam Richiardi, Lauren Rosier, Rhys Thomas
Jacket Designer David McDonald
Senior DTP Designer Kavita Varma
Pre-production Producer Siu Chan
Producer Lloyd Robertson
Managing Editor Simon Hugo
Design Manager Guy Harvey
Creative Manager Sarah Harland
Art Director Lisa Lanzarini
Publisher Julie Ferris
Publishing Director Simon Beecroft

For the LEGO Group
Project Manager Mikkel Joachim Petersen
Assistant Licensing Manager Randi Kirsten Sørensen
Senior Licensing Manager Corinna van Delden
Designer Melody Louise Caddick
Building Instruction Developer Alexandra Martin
Model makers Stephen Berry, Yvonne Doyle, Rod Gillies, Tim Goddard, Tim Johnson, Barney Main, Pete Reid

Photography by Gary Ombler

First published in the United States in 2015 by DK Publishing
345 Hudson Street, New York, New York 10014

Contains material previously published in LEGO® *Play Book* (2013)

003—284611—Mar/15

Page design copyright © 2015 Dorling Kindersley Limited.
A Penguin Random House Company.

Acknowledgments
Dorling Kindersley would like to thank: Randi Sørensen, Mikkel Petersen, Melody Caddick, Corinna van Delden, and Alexandra Martin at the LEGO Group; Stephen Berry, Yvonne Doyle, Rod Gillies, Tim Goddard, Tim Johnson, Barney Main, Pete Reid, and Andrew Walker for their amazing models; Daniel Lipkowitz for his inspiring text; Gary Ombler for his endless patience and brilliant photography; and Emma Grange, Lauren Nesworthy, Lisa Stock, and Matt Wilson for editorial and design assistance.

A WORLD OF IDEAS:
SEE ALL THERE IS TO KNOW

1x1 brick x 7

4x6 plate x 1

1x1 headlight brick x 2

1x4 brick x 6

1x2 brick x 5
(including 1 transparent)

1x6 brick x 2

2x3 brick x 1

1x2 jumper plate x 3

1x2x1 panel x1

1x1 round plate x 2

1x4 plate x 2

2x2 radar dish x 2

Wide rim, wide tire, and 2x2 axle plate with 1 pin x 4

2x6 plate x 3

1x1 plate x 4

1x2 grille plate x 2

2x4 plate x 2

Faucet x 1

1x6 arch brick x 1

2x2 round plate x 2

4x4 radar dish x 1